At the Pond

Werner Zimmermann

North Winds Press
An Imprint of Scholastic Canada Ltd.

The paintings for this book were created in watercolour on Arches 90 lb hot press paper.

Library and Archives Canada Cataloguing in Publication

Zimmermann, H. Werner (Heinz Werner), 1951-, author
    At the pond / Werner Zimmermann.

ISBN 978-1-4431-4287-8 (hardcover)

    1. Counting--Juvenile literature. 2. Numbers, Natural--Juvenile literature. 3. Fishes--Juvenile literature. 4. Pond ecology--Juvenile literature. I. Title.

QA113.Z56 2018   j513.2'11   C2018-901235-8

www.scholastic.ca

6 5 4 3 2 1   Printed in Malaysia 108   18 19 20 21 22

To my granddaughter Vivienne for inspiration, and to my wife, Lori, for love.

One fish,

Two fish,

Three fish,

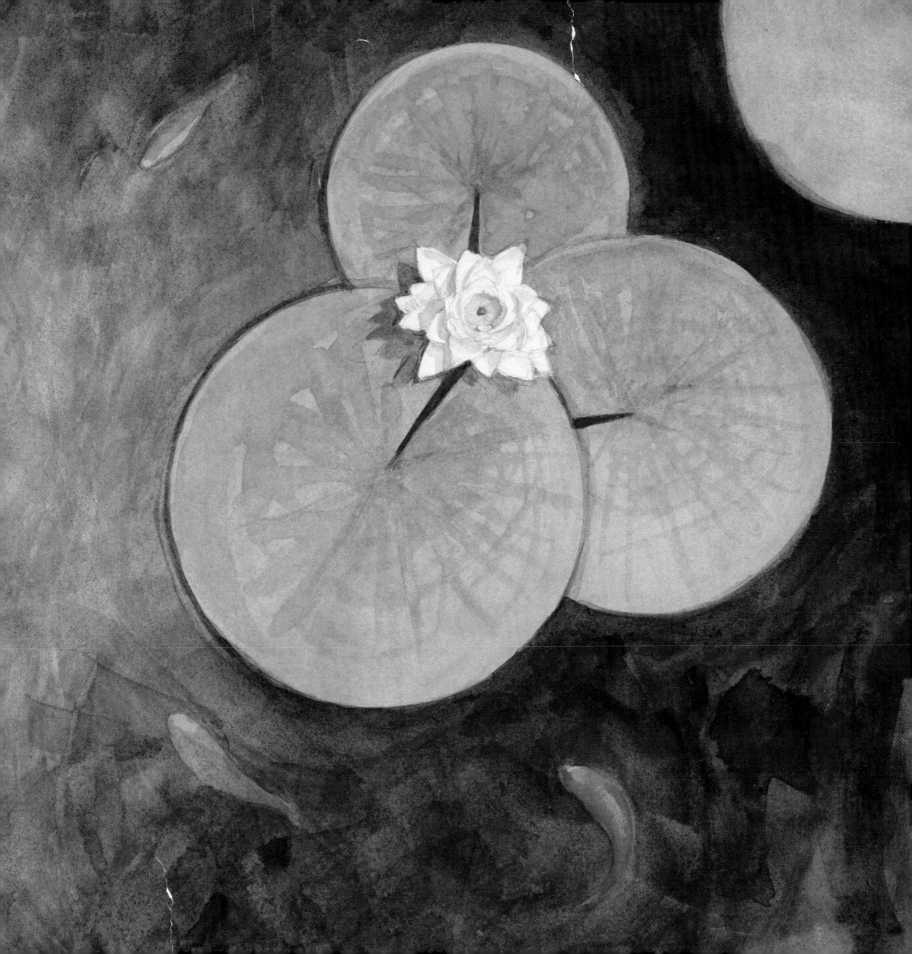

Four.

Five fish,

Six fish,

Seven fish,

More?

Eight fish,

Nine fish,

Ten fish,

Then . . .

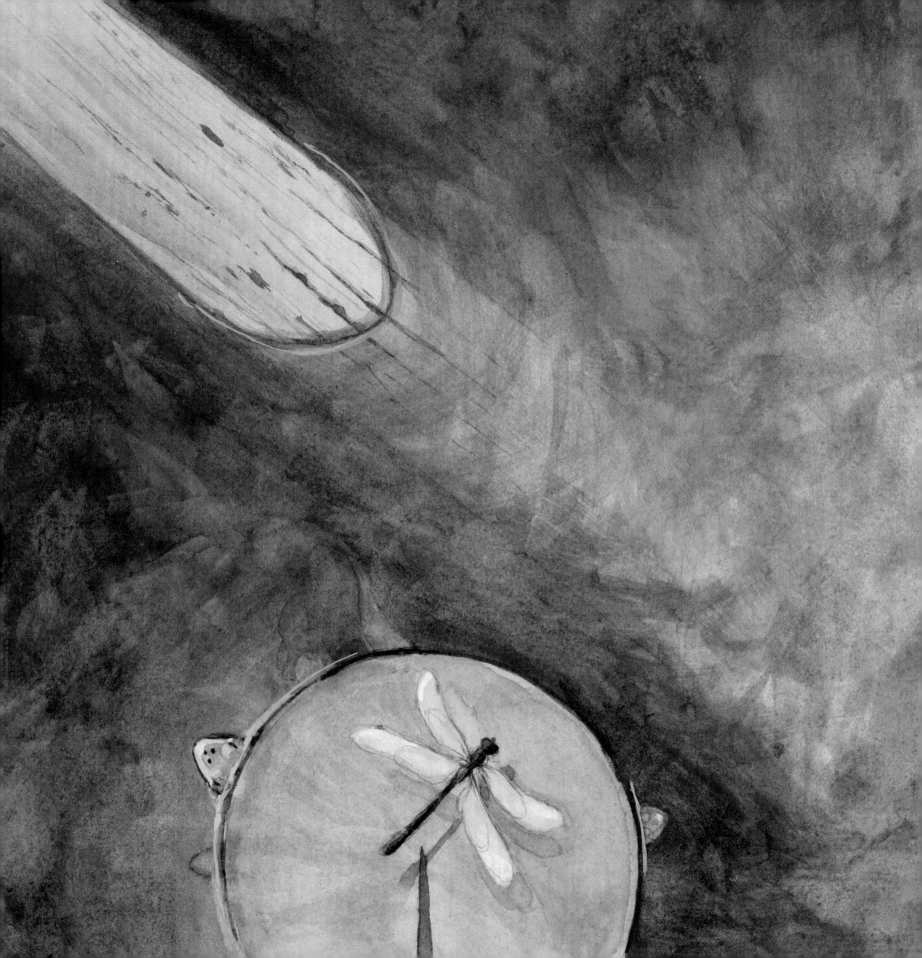

We start to count them
all over again!

What's in the pond?

The **fragrant white water lily** grows across North America. Its large round leaves and flowers float on top of ponds and other still water, and its stalk extends downward into the mud at the bottom. The flowers open in the morning and close in the afternoon, or earlier on very cloudy days.

The bright orange **common goldfish** is a tiny member of the carp family. It is a popular fish for aquariums and backyard ponds. Originally from East Asia, the goldfish was introduced to North America by settlers more than 300 years ago.

Northern leopard frogs live in many habitats, and they seek out slow-moving water such as ponds to lay their eggs. They eat spiders and insects and rely on their speed to escape from predators such as herons, raccoons and large fish. In the winter they hibernate at the bottom of deep ponds that do not freeze solid.

The **mourning dove**'s distinctive coo can be heard across southern Canada. Mourning doves usually nest in trees or shrubs, where females lay two eggs at a time and raise up to six broods a year. They eat mostly seeds, but sometimes snack on grasses, berries and snails.

Common water striders are also called pond skaters and water skippers. They use surface tension to skitter across still water on their six water-repellent legs, keeping in constant motion to avoid predators. They eat mosquito larvae that live under the surface of the water, grasping their prey with their front legs.

Lilypad clubtail dragonflies are about five centimetres long and eat mostly insects. The males are dark green with black stripes, and the females are yellowish with black markings. Their large eyes are blue-green. They are speedy flyers, and as their name suggests, they like to rest on lilypads!

A **great blue heron** can have a wingspan of up to two metres. It can be found in marshes and beaver ponds, standing in shallow water and keeping a sharp eye out for fish and amphibians to snap up. Although great blue herons hunt alone, they often nest in large colonies with many nests high up in each tree.

Spotted salamanders are black or dark brown, with large yellow or orange spots running in two lines down their backs. Adults can grow up to 25 centimetres long, and can regrow a limb or tail if they lose one to a predator! They are rarely seen because they spend most of the day hiding underground or under logs, and hibernate during the winter.